TESTIMONY

of a

TAX COLLECTOR

E. K. Bailey

MOODY PUBLISHERS
CHICAGO

© 2004 by
E. K. BAILEY

All rights reserved. No part of this book may be reproduced in any form without permission in writing from the publisher, except in the case of brief quotations embodied in critical articles or reviews.

Text design and illustrations by Coffee Bean Design

Cover Design: The Smartt Guys

Cover Photo: © 2004 Ronald Bude

Library of Congress Cataloging-in-Publication Data

Bailey, E. K., 1945-
    Testimony of a tax collector / by E.K. Bailey.
        p. cm.
    Includes bibliographical references.
    ISBN 0-8024-3732-X
    1. Zacchaeus (Biblical character) I. Title.

BS2520.Z3B35 2004
226.4'09505--dc22

                                        2003027291

1 3 5 7 9 10 8 6 4 2

Printed in the United States of America

How I Met the Tax Collector

One of the many benefits children experience growing up in a local church is the various assortment of songs, rhymes, games, and couplets that indelibly stamp the names of biblical characters upon the fabric of their minds. When I was a young boy, I learned the following rhyme, one I still recall today:

> Zacchaeus was a wee little man,
>
> A wee little man was he.
>
> He climbed up in a sycamore tree,
>
> For the Lord he wanted to see.
>
> But as the Savior passed that way
>
> He looked up in the tree,
>
> And He said,
>
> "Zacchaeus, you come down,
>
> For I'm going to your house today."[1]

That's how I first met the tax collector. Since then, I've always wondered what drove Zacchaeus to climb that tree. What was his motivation? For it is exceedingly unusual, imaginatively unlikely, and totally uncanny to see a well-dressed, well-educated, well-established, wealthy man at midday publicly but shamelessly climbing a tree, crawling out on its branches, hanging on a limb.

So at times I wonder: *What led Zacchaeus to ignore embarrassment, disregard shame, reject ridicule, and do something as uncharacteristic as climbing a tree for all to see?*

In order to answer these and other questions, I invite you to take a journey with me. We must travel to the backside of the Roman Empire, penetrate the sweltering, fly-infested land of Palestine, traverse the difficult terrain of the Holy Land, and then enter the fragrance-filled city of Jericho, where we will find the home of this despicable and despised tax collector named Zacchaeus.

TESTIMONY

of a

TAX COLLECTOR

ZACCHAEUS ROSE EARLY EACH MORNING for a full day of calling on the residents of Jericho, who all owed taxes.

He pulled out his day planner to check the names and addresses of the people he wanted to see that day.

It wasn't long before he arrived at his first scheduled appointment. He noticed that it was an unkempt, dilapidated shanty, desperately in need of some paint and major repairs. There would be no sympathy or mercy coming from Zacchaeus.

THE ONLY THING THAT WAS OF ANY
IMPORTANCE WAS THE WORD

STAMPED BY THE PERSON'S NAME.

HE KNOCKED ON THE DOOR.

As the door swung open, it creaked and groaned with the eeriness of an Alfred Hitchcock movie. On the other side stood a frail, blind man.

The blind man asked,

"Who's there?"

And the answer came, "Zacchaeus. I'm here to collect the taxes you owe the Roman government."

In a trembling voice, the blind man began to explain his inability to pay his taxes.

"I have no family," he said. "I don't receive any pension. And there's no society dedicated to helping the blind. I want to pay you, but right now I am not able to pay. But, please, I beg you, have mercy, Mr. Zacchaeus."

GIVE ME THIRTY DAYS. I DON'T KNOW
HOW OR WHERE, BUT SOMEHOW I'LL
FIND THE MONEY."

Zacchaeus was caught between money and mercy. He told the blind man, "That's not usually my style, but you have thirty days.

BUT, BLIND MAN, WHEN I GET BACK, IF YOU DON'T SHOW ME THE MONEY, YOU'LL NOT ONLY BE BLIND, BUT YOU'LL BE HOMELESS."

Zacchaeus turned, and as he walked away he thought,

That didn't go very well. Perhaps I'll have better luck at the next house

He came to his next appointment and pounded ferociously on the door. As the woman slowly opened the door, Zacchaeus grimaced as he immediately recognized that there was going to be a problem.

The woman's complexion was completely discolored. It was whitish-yellow, as if all the blood had been drained from her face. Her eyes seemed as if they were being sucked out of their sockets, her lips were cracked and swollen, her cheekbones were disfigured and repulsively protruded from her face, and her hair was dry, trashy, and matted. Her face was wet with tears.

Her speech was slurred as she said, "I know who you are and why you've come. But, Mr. Zacchaeus . . . Oh, Mr. Zacchaeus, I don't have any way of paying my taxes.

You see, for twelve years I've had a blood disorder. In that time, my husband divorced me and I lost all my health benefits. Now I have no savings or any money to pay my bills, and I have even pawned my jewelry and sold all my furniture and everything in my checking account is spent.

BUT GIVE ME THIRTY DAYS—
JUST THIRTY DAYS. ALL I NEED
IS AT LEAST THIRTY DAYS."

Zacchaeus was caught between greed and grace. He said, "For some reason I feel benevolent today. You have thirty days. But when I return, I want the taxes." As he walked away he thought, *Maybe I'll have better luck at the next house.*

As Zacchaeus walked around the bend, he spotted the third house. A woman stood listless and almost catatonic in front of the house. She stared into space, not seeming to recognize that he was moving closer to her. When he tried to speak to her, there was no response.

SUDDENLY, HE HEARD A SPINE-CHILLING
SCREAM COME FROM BEHIND HIM.

Zacchaeus turned sharply to see where the
scream came from. On the hillside across the
street, running nude between the stones in the
graveyard, was the silhouette of what looked
like a cross between a man and a beast, reck-
lessly wounding himself.

Now the woman in front of the house broke her silence. "That man was once my husband," she said. "He was a good man. I'm still praying that one day he'll be restored and return to his family. Some have suggested that I should move on with my life, but I still love him. He's the father of my children. I'm not sure if it will ever happen, because no man can tame him and no man can bind him.

HE CALLS HIMSELF LEGION BECAUSE
HE'S POSSESSED BY MANY DEMONS,"
she added.

NOW ZACCHAEUS WAS CAUGHT
BETWEEN DOLLARS AND DEMONS.

Not anxious to dialogue with demons, Zacchaeus began to retrace his steps. Before the woman said anything about the taxes, Zacchaeus said, "I'll be back in your area in thirty days. Be prepared to pay upon my return."

He hurriedly turned away, his heart still palpitating. He looked at his day planner and noted there was one last house to visit. When he arrived, there was a funeral ornament hanging on the door, suggesting that someone had died. But not even a family tragedy would stop Zacchaeus, so he knocked anyway. A grieving woman, veiled and dressed in black, answered the door.

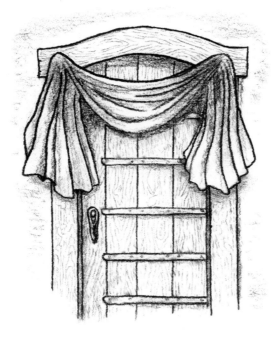

"I know who you are and why you've come," she said. "Zacchaeus, my son died yesterday, and I'm on my way to the funeral.

I HAD TO USE
THE TAX MONEY
TO BURY MY
ONLY SON."

"I've already given some of your neighbors thirty days," Zacchaeus said. "So I'll be back in thirty days." Now Zacchaeus was trapped between the law and love.

The thirty days passed quickly. Zacchaeus left home at the crack of dawn, as he did every day. He opened his day planner and noticed that this was the day he was to return to those four homes—those houses that represented the most unproductive day in his career as a tax collector.

He squared his shoulders, and as he walked he said aloud to himself and anyone who might overhear,

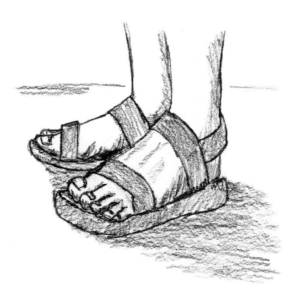

"NO SOB STORY WILL DISSUADE
ME TODAY. THEY WILL EITHER PAY,
SURRENDER THEIR PROPERTY, OR BE
THROWN IN PRISON."

At the first house he noticed a significant change. The grass had been manicured. The house had undergone extensive renovation. He knocked on the door. Zacchaeus became mesmerized when he saw the man who answered the door. He had a piercing gaze and a voice that boomed with authority.

"I'm sorry, sir, but I'm looking for the man of the house. The blind man."

"I AM THE MAN OF THE HOUSE."

"No," Zacchaeus replied, "I was here thirty days ago, and the man I spoke with was blind."

"I'm that man. I was blind.

Mr. Zacchaeus, let me explain to you my story. One day a man told me that Jesus was coming to our town and so I ran to the town square so that I could see him. I knew it might be my only chance to meet Him. When Jesus was passing by, I heard all the commotion.

I asked, 'What's happening?'

They said, 'Jesus is passing by.'

And I yelled,

> 'JESUS, SON OF DAVID,
> HAVE MERCY ON ME!'

"The townspeople, the city leaders, and religious leaders—they all said, 'Hush, you're making a nuisance of yourself. You're embarrassing the town.'

"But I cried louder,

> 'JESUS! SON OF DAVID,
> HAVE MERCY ON ME!'

"Then they tried to silence me,
but I knew this was my only chance.

I cried louder still—

> 'JESUS, SON OF DAVID,
> HAVE MERCY ON ME!'"

The man looked directly at the tax collector and asked, "Zacchaeus, do you have time? Sit down and let me tell you about what happened, for I have a testimony to tell. This is the way it was:

> *"Amazing grace, how sweet the sound*
>
> *That saved a wretch like me.*
>
> *I once was lost, but now I'm found*
>
> *I was blind, but now I see."*[2]

As Zacchaeus walked away, he thought, *This is some day! A man who was blind can now see.* Inside his day planner were the coins from the once-blind man. Zacchaeus mused, *One day I hope I will meet Jesus. Maybe Jesus can do something about my condition. That man had said that this world's god has blinded the minds of unbelievers so they cannot see the light of the gospel of the glory of Christ, who is the image of God.*

Zacchaeus muttered aloud,

"I HOPE I CAN SEE JESUS SOMEDAY,"

Upon arriving at the second house, he knocked on the door, and a beautiful woman, radiant with joy, answered. She had color in her cheeks, a sparkle in her eyes. She had a new hairdo. Yes, she was stylish. Her nails had been freshly manicured.

"Mr. Zacchaeus," she said, "it's good to see you." She was smiling effortlessly, even glamorously.

"I'm looking for the woman of the house," Zacchaeus said.

"I am the woman of the house," she said.

"Wait a minute. . . Do you know your blind neighbor down the street?"

"Yes, I know him. But he's not blind anymore."

"I know," Zacchaeus said. "He paid his taxes today."

"Yes, and he's sold his guide dog," she added.

"Zacchaeus, when I told you to come back thirty days ago, that was only a ploy. I was confident that in thirty days I would be dead. In fact, I had been praying to die. I thought that only death could deliver me from this unbearable existence. But a friend told me that Jesus was coming to town.

"I elbowed my way through the suffocating crowd. When I got close enough, I stretched out and was just able to touch the hem of His garment. And the moment I touched Him, the blood that had been flowing for twelve years immediately dried up! BUT NOT ONLY WAS MY BODY HEALED, MY SOUL WAS MADE WHOLE. EVEN THOUGH MY FAITH WAS INADEQUATE, HE MADE IT SUFFICIENT."

"I don't know how much of this I can take
. . . a blind man who can see, a dying woman
who's full of life. . ."

"Zacchaeus, I know it's hard to believe, but
I need to tell you what happened."

"I've had some good days. I've had some
      hills to climb.

I've had some weary days and some
      sleepless nights.

But when I look around and think things
      over,

All of my good days outweigh my bad days,
      I won't complain.

The Lord has been good to me; He's been so
      good to me,

More than this old world could ever be.
      He's been good to me!"[3]

"Zacchaeus, no more doctor bills and no more prescriptions to fill. I've been able to save a little money. Like my old ex-blind friend, here's the money for your taxes."

Zacchaeus turned sharply and headed toward the third house. He thought, *This is a weird and wacky day. I wonder if I will ever meet Jesus. Like that woman, I've had*

*some longstanding, ever-present problems.
I've had some painful experiences. Maybe if
I could meet Jesus, He could do something
about my problems.*

Soon he was in front of that third house. He looked for the woman to be standing at the front of the house, but she was not there. When he knocked on the door, the woman answered. But before they could start talking, a handsome young man walked out from behind her. Zacchaeus' first thought was,

I'm glad this woman got a new man. She should have kicked that old grave dweller to the curb.

About the same time, the woman spoke up. "Mr. Zacchaeus, I want you to meet my husband. You haven't met this man, because when you were here thirty days ago, his home was in the graveyard. But look at him now. Doesn't he look good? He's clothed and in his right mind.

"Mr. Zacchaeus, I owe you an apology. Thirty days ago I told you that no man could tame him, no man could bind him, but that was before Jesus stepped off the boat. When Jesus walked in, the demons walked out. Look at him. He's a new man!

"Mr. Zacchaeus, if you want to be a new man, go meet Jesus. He will change your life forever and make you to be a new and better man. Old things will pass away, and all things will become new. My husband met Jesus, and his life has been forever changed."

"Wait a minute!" Her husband cut in. "She can tell the story, but it is my testimony as well, and she didn't experience it like I experienced it. Sit down, Zacchaeus. You can't stand up and listen to this. I need to tell you what happened."

"*I know I've been changed*

I know I've been changed

I know I've been changed

The angels in heaven done signed my name

I know I've been changed . . . "[4]

The husband finished his song, and then he paid the tax collector.

As Zacchaeus left, he thought, *A blind man who can now see, a dying, helpless woman who's now healed and full of life, and a demon-possessed man who has been delivered. Now I wonder if some day I will ever meet Jesus. I've got some demons hounding my heels. Maybe if I meet Jesus, I too will be delivered.*

At the last house he thought rather sarcastically, *I wonder what surprise they will have for me.* When he knocked on the door, the cutest little boy with the widest smile opened the door.

"I'm sorry. I'm at the wrong house," said Zacchaeus. "There is no little boy that lives in the house that I'm looking for. Ironically, thirty days ago the woman of the house was on her way to bury her only son."

"Are you Mr. Zacchaeus?" the boy said. "Mama's been expecting you. She said that you'd be back in thirty days. And Mama said you're never late collecting taxes."

Zacchaeus was startled. His heartbeat surged, and blood rushed to his head. He paused and gazed steadily at the boy, and then

he tersely said, "Wait a minute. This could never be the house where that little boy died."

The boy said,

"MR. ZACCHAEUS, I'M THAT BOY.

I died. My mama's worst fear was that the disease that took my daddy and my older brother would some day take me. And thirty days ago my mama's worst fear came true. I got real sick. And my mother prayed for me. She stayed by my bedside all day and all night. But God chose not to heal me, and I died. My mother saved the money to pay you, but she had to use that money on my funeral."

The young boy seemed to know all that happened. He continued. "As the mourners led the procession out of Nain, there was another procession going in. And the procession of death collided with the procession of deity. Now, Mr. Zach, you know that death and deity cannot occupy the same space. You know that Jesus never just attended a funeral.

He never preached at a funeral. Every time He showed up, He transformed the funeral into a resurrection. And there we were at the gate . . . death versus deity.

"You should have seen the fireworks when death collided with deity! Jesus laid His resurrecting hand on me, and suddenly something began to stir in my lifeless body. I came back to life, Mr. Zach! When I sat up in the casket, it scared the undertaker so bad that he pushed me on out of the casket, took his casket back, and gave my mother her money back.

"Mr. Zach, here's the money for your taxes."

By the time the little boy finished talking, his mama came out. She said, "He's only twelve. He doesn't know much about life's deeper realities, so let me tell you like only a mama can tell you. Sit down. Do you have a little time, Mr. Zacchaeus? Let me tell you what happened."

"Yes, tell me what happened," he said.

The mother began her story with a song of praise:

> *"Great is Thy faithfulness, O God my Father*
>
> *There is no shadow of turning with thee*
>
> *Thou changest not, Thy compassions, they fail not*
>
> *As Thou has been Thou forever will be.*
>
> *Great is Thy faithfulness! Morning by morning new mercies I see*
>
> *All I have needed Thy hand hath provided*
>
> *Great is Thy faithfulness, Lord, unto me."*[5]

When Zacchaeus left, he thought, *A blind man who can see, a dying woman who's full of life, a demon-possessed man who has been delivered, and a dead boy that's been resurrected. Amazing!*

Zacchaeus closed his day planner. On his way home, he passed a friend. "Hey, Zach, have you heard?"

"I've heard all I can handle for one day."

"Hey, Jesus is in town!"

"He is?! I NEED TO SEE HIM. . . I MUST SEE HIM!"

"You'd better hurry. He'll be leaving soon."

And as his little feet pitter-pattered along the dusty road, Zacchaeus pondered about all his life experiences. And he mumbled:

"I wonder if this is my chance to meet Jesus. All of my life I've been a successful failure. I've been a paradox of prosperity and poverty. I'm rich in the things of this world but poor in the things of God.

"I've had a tough and terrible life," Zacchaeus muttered. "At a glance I look like the fulfillment of every man's dream. But what people don't know is that sometimes when you get to the top of the ladder you discover that it's leaning against the wrong building."

He sighed, and then said softly, "MAYBE JESUS CAN DO SOMETHING ABOUT THE EMPTINESS THAT FILLS MY SOUL."

And then he admitted another problem that had pursued him through his adult years. "I've been a short man in a tall world, and I'm always thinking that the shortness of my stature has created all of my problems. But maybe if I meet Jesus, He will help me to understand who I really am. Because

I'm beginning to see as I search my heart that it's not the shortness of my stature, but it's the shortness of my relationship with God that has caused me to be so cold, callous, and uncompassionate. Maybe if I meet Jesus He will change my heart and my life."

So he ran to the town. When he got there, he couldn't see over the dense crowd. So finally he decided to run ahead of Jesus and the crowd. And as he ran he saw that sycamore tree. Why did he choose to climb that tree? Not because of the shortness of his stature, but because his seething soul could find sufficiency and satisfaction only in the Savior. Also, Zacchaeus climbed that tree because he remembered what Jesus had done in the lives of other people . . . and he was utterly aware of the urgent changes that needed to occur in his own life.

As though this was a scene from a Spider Man story, Zacchaeus stretched and slung himself at that tree, and with a single leap, he lunged up that tree.

Jesus came by and saw him and said, "Zacchaeus, you come down, for I'm going to your house today."

Isn't it good to know that Jesus knows what tree you are up and what limb you are on? And He will call you down!

Zacchaeus slid down his tree of despair, Zacchaeus slid down his tree of pride, and Zacchaeus slid down his tree of guilt and

decided for the rest of his life that he would walk with Jesus.

Zacchaeus' first thought at the foot of the tree was, *I've got to invite Him home with me, because Jesus always makes a difference when He goes home with you.*

In fact, if Jesus doesn't go home with you, He doesn't go anywhere with you—because Jesus knows who you are, who you really are, when you are at home.

As Zacchaeus walked away with his arm around Jesus, I could hear him singing,

"*Jesus saves to the utmost*

He will pick you up, and He'll turn you around

Hallelujah . . . yes, Jesus saves."[6]

NOTES

1. "Zacchaeus." Words by Elsie Leslie. In public domain.

2. "Amazing Grace." Words by John Newton. In public domain.

3. "I Won't Complain." Words by James Lennox.

4. "Lord, I Know I Have Been Changed. Traditional spiritual. In public domain.

5. "Great Is Thy Faithfulness." Words by Thomas O. Chilsolm. Music by William M. Runyon. © 1923, renewed 1951 Hope Publishing Company, Carol Stream, IL 60188. All rights reserved. International copyright secured. Used by permission.

6. "Jesus Saves." Words by James Cleveland. Copyright 1963.

About the Author

E. K. Bailey (D.Min., United Theological Seminary), one of this century's premiere preachers, was born in Marshall, Texas, on December 19, 1945. He established the Concord Missionary Baptist Church in Dallas, Texas in 1975. He dedicated his life to the preaching of the Gospel and devoted his ministerial skills to the enablement of change for the disenfranchised. He had a great love for expository preaching and was a mentor to many a preacher and pastor. He founded E. K. Bailey Ministries, Inc. to facilitate several conferences toward this end, including the Institute on Church Growth. He served for twenty-eight years as senior pastor for the Concord Missionary Baptist Church where he preached many powerful, life-changing sermons. E. K. Bailey went to be with the Lord on October 22, 2003 and is survived by his wife Sheila and their three children.

Since 1894, Moody Publishers has been dedicated to equip and motivate people to advance the cause of Christ by publishing evangelical Christian literature and other media for all ages, around the world. Because we are a ministry of the Moody Bible Institute of Chicago, a portion of the proceeds from the sale of this book go to train the next generation of Christian leaders.

If we may serve you in any way in your spiritual journey toward understanding Christ and the Christian life, please contact us at www.moodypublishers.com.

"All Scripture is God-breathed and is useful for teaching, rebuking, correcting and training in righteousness, so that the man of God may be thoroughly equipped for every good work."

—2 TIMOTHY 3:16, 17

MOODY
PUBLISHERS

THE NAME YOU CAN TRUST®